3.

AUSTRALIA

Designed and Produced by

Ted Smart & David Gibbon

MAYFLOWER BOOKS · NEW YORK CITY

Introduction:

AUSTRALIA is an island continent about the size of Western Europe, or the United States of America excluding Alaska. Geographically one of the world's oldest land masses, Australia's three million square miles contain a fantastic range of natural features, flora and fauna. It is the only continent occupied solely by one nation. More than a third of it is tropical and yet there are huge snowfields, and most of its 14.2 million inhabitants live along the eastern and southern coasts and in the south-west corner of the continent. All but one of Australia's major cities are on the coast and all have a cosmopolitan flavour, the result of years of migration, largely from Europe.

Australians think big in terms of distance – they have to. Their country measures approximately 2,500 miles from east to west and 2,000 miles from north to south and its extensive shoreline is washed by the waters of four seas and three oceans.

Such distances are, however, minimised by efficient air, rail and road networks. Sydney, on the east coast, to Perth on the west coast occupies only a little over four hours flying time or, at a more leisurely pace, the Indian Pacific Railway completes the trans-continental journey – the third longest rail journey in the world – in three scenically fascinating days.

The continent contains great deserts and lush farmlands, mighty rivers, inland seas which disappear in times of drought, vast and wierd geological formations in areas remote from civilisation, and bustling, booming, clean, modern cities.

Off the Queensland coast, to the north-east, is the Great Barrier Reef, the largest of its kind in the world; the chain of some 600 islands and islets stretching for about 1,250 miles. Beneath the warm waters – and sometimes exposed at low tide – is a fairyland composed of scores of different types of coral and many varieties of tropical fish.

Away from the cities lies the Great Outback of Australia. Still one of the most thinly-populated areas on earth, this is where the famous 'flying doctor' operates and where children carry out their school lessons with the help of radio – the 'school of the air'.

Australia is a country where farming and grazing properties are huge – some covering about 20,000 square miles – with prairies of wheat stretching far over the horizon and where, in the tropics, there are miles of pineapple plantations and banana groves.

There are children in the cities and coastal towns and villages who learn to swim and surf ride almost as soon as they can walk – and sometimes before. Yet there are others, in the Outback, to whom the sea is unknown.

Such is this country of contrasts, which varies from tropics to snow. Most of the people – about four fifths – live in the capital cities of the states and in a few large provincial cities.

Threequarters of the population of Australia was born there, and the rest are migrants from all over the world, but largely Europe and predominantly Britain. They came at first as unwilling settlers – convicts transported from Britain as she emptied her overcrowded prison hulks and jails of some 160,000 offenders. They were soon far outnumbered, however, by free settlers eager for land, and then by prospectors eager for gold.

Gold was first discovered in Bendigo and Ballarat, Central Victoria, in 1853. Within ten years the population of Australia jumped from 400,000 to 1,400,000 – mostly lured by the gold fever and land hunger.

Although gold was responsible for the first great rush, capturing as it did the imaginations of adventurers throughout the world, migration has been far greater since, especially in the years following the Second World War.

It is now known that the Australian earth contains far greater riches than would ever have been dreamed of by the early gold pioneers. There are vast deposits of brown and black coal, lead, zinc, copper, bauxite and many other minerals and the offshore oilfields supply most of the country's needs. Some of Australia's mines are among the world's largest and there are extensive processing and manufacturing industries in areas where population is centred. Despite this, Australia is still a significant producer of wheat, dairy produce, meat, sugar and fruit and a high degree of mechanisation is employed.

Although Australia is the oldest continent it is also, in some ways, one of the 'newest' in the sense that it is a European civilisation set down between the Indian and Pacific Oceans. For some 1,500 years it was referred to as 'Terra Australis Incognita' – the Unknown South Land.

The exact date of Australia's discovery is uncertain. The Dutch mapped part of the northern coast as early as 1606, but there are theories that suggest the Portuguese were there even earlier. Britain's Captain James Cook discovered and charted Australia's east coast in 1770 and eight years later a convict settlem

Page 4. Reminders of Australia's pioneering past can be found all over the country. This old horse-drawn buggy lies where it was abandoned years ago, on the edge of a creek in southern Victoria.

was established on the site of present-day Sydney. By the end of the 19th century Australia consisted of six separate colonies. Federation was proclaimed by Queen Victoria in 1900 and Australia became a self-governing nation. It still has strong ties with Britain, however, and a Governor General represents the Queen in Canberra, with State Governors in each of the State capital cities. Today there are six States and seven Territories, with Canberra, which is situated between the major cities of Melbourne and Sydney, the modern Federal capital.

Despite two centuries of settlement and development, there are still areas on maps of Australia which are marked 'largely unexplored' and exploration for minerals still continues today. Recent archeological discoveries suggest that Australia was first settled by 'island hopping' peoples from South East Asia about 30,000 years ago. Some rock and cave carvings have been carbon dated to about this time. It is also believed that there were hundreds of different tribal groupings and languages as the nomadic Aborigines spread throughout the continent.

Remote and isolated from the rest of the world, Australia's plants and animals evolved in their own unique way, adapting to the continent's range of climatic conditions. There are flightless birds – emus – and those beloved 'teddy bears' – the koalas – which aren't bears at all but marsupials. One of nature's strangest creatures is the platypus, also known as the duckbill or duckmole, an egg-laying, amphibious mammal which suckles its young and has venomous barbs on its hind legs, and looks something like a cross between a duck and a beaver! Then, of course, there is the kangaroo, together with its many relations, ranging in size from one to six or even eight feet in height. In the Northern Territory there are also great herds of wild water buffalo, imported from Timor by early settlers as beasts of burden, and wild horses, camels and goats. There are tree ferns in the rain forests that stand taller than a man, crocodiles and sharks which adapted to freshwater when inland seas drained, and earthworms which grow up to six feet in length. Both gum trees – eucalyptus – and wattles – acacia – have about 600 species and giant mushrooms can be found which measure up to three feet across and, particularly in Western Australia, there is the world's greatest collection of wildflowers.

_____lia's bird life ranges from parakeets to ___t flocks of cockatoos can cast racing ___he dry, red earth of the continent's ___ustralia's most famous birds is the ___ra, a member of the kingfisher ___ dancing lyrebird, a superb mimic

of other birds and all forest noises – it will even imitate the clunk of an axe or the buzz of a chain saw. Also among Australia's 736 recorded species are eagles and honeyeaters.

Today, it is possible to drive right round Australia, mostly on sealed roads, but there are still frontiers to be tamed in the Great Outback, albeit with the aid of modern technology such as computers and air conditioning, and there are thousands of square miles of national parks, largely untouched by man. It is still possible to follow the tracks of the great Victorian explorers and, in some areas, to see re-creations of pioneering settlements or gold mining villages of the early days.

The Centre of Australia is unique. The Great Outback, one of the last places on earth where the wonders of nature have remained untouched by man seems to stretch over limitless horizons and here, sprouting from the red, sunlit plain and its wavering mirages, is Ayers Rock, the world's largest monolith, five miles in circumference and 1,100 feet high. This is only the tip of a huge mountain, however, which fell on its side during the early days of the earth's creation. As the sun rises and sets the massive rock changes colour from brown to brilliant red, purple and black – an awesome sight. It is small wonder that the rock was held to be sacred by the Aborigines, who depicted their legends in galleries of rock paintings at its base. Nearby are the Mount Olga Ranges, a series of vividly-coloured rock domes and, away to the north lies Cairns, a famous big game fishing centre and a mecca for wealthy deep-sea fishermen. To the south is Australia's island state – Tasmania – wild, rugged and a paradise for trout fishermen.

Wherever the visitor travels in Australia there is evidence that the people are fond of the outdoors and of sports of all kinds: football, cricket, tennis, horse racing, sailing, surfing and swimming and that they love festivals – such as Melbourne's annual Moomba ('let's get together and have fun') and the biennial Adelaide Arts Festival which alternates with the Barossa Valley Vintage Wine Festival.

This big land has long been called 'the lucky country,' with its natural and man-made marvels and its friendly, outgoing people. It is a country of fine wines, colour, exotic sea foods and huge steaks. It is a country that combines the ancient and the new, and which is symbolised for many people by the white 'sails' of Sydney Opera House, overlooking one of the world's greatest and most beautiful harbours.

Australia's 23,000 mile coastline is washed by four seas and three oceans. Overleaf is pictured the South Pacific pounding the NSW coast.

Austra...
penguins. Grea...
shadows over t...
'centre'. One of A...
laughing kookabur...
family; another is the...

Although it was in fact the last of Australia's cities to be built, Canberra, as the national capital, lays claim to the title of first city. This position was previously held by Melbourne and it was not until 1927 that Canberra was inaugurated. Canberra is, and was always intended as, a showplace city, with landscape and architecture blending to form a harmonious whole. The city, which is crossed by the Molongo River, lives on an upland plain 150 miles south west of Sydney.

A terrestial globe top left on the shores of Lake Burley Griffin marks the bi-centenary of Captain Cook's discovery of eastern Australia. The structure acts as a pointer to a water jet in the lake which can send columns of water shooting to a height of 137 metres in the air.

The view centre left was taken from inside the entrances to the law courts in Canberra. In the foreground is shown the back of the coat of arms.

Parliament House bottom left is set among trees, lawns, rose gardens and fountains. It has been the provisional seat of the Federal Parliament since 1927, when the opening ceremony was performed by the Duke of York. It has not yet been decided where the permanent building will be situated but the choice will probably be made beween the shore of Lake Burley Griffin and the hub of the city plan, Capital Hill.

The impressive geometrical layout pictured right features ANZAC Parade, which sweeps from the Australian War Memorial in the foreground to the lake, with beyond, the broad vista leading to Parliament House.

The huge expanse of Lake Burley Griffin dominates the view overleaf. The artificial lake was named after the architect of Canberra, the American Walter Burley Griffin.

Commemorating the contribution of the American people to the defence of Australia during the Second World War is the Australian-American Memorial above.

Left is pictured Australia's Royal Military College, Duntroon. Tidbinbilla space tracking station below is situated about 25 miles from Canberra and is open for public tours.

Bottom is shown the Captain Cook memorial water jet in Lake Burley Griffin.

A typical sheep-farming scene is pictured top right.

Canberra's St John's Church and its setting bottom right could have come straight from an English country village.

Sydney's skyscrapers reach into the sky overleaf.

The famous 'coathanger' bridge left and below *still spans Sydney Harbour as it has since its opening in 1932, but it has now been overshadowed by the acclaim accorded the incredibly beautiful Opera House above, right and below.*

Sydney Opera House, built on the shores of Sydney Harbour, was paid for by twice-weekly lotteries and is one of the most controversial buildings ever constructed in Australia. Its gull winged shape contrasts strongly with the angularity of buildings in downtown Sydney overleaf. Circular Quay, the ferry terminal, may be seen to the right of and behind the Opera House. On the right of the picture is the P and O liner Canberra.

In the interior shot of the Opera House below right *may be seen the doughnut-shaped 'flying saucers' which are, in fact, designed to improve the acoustics.*

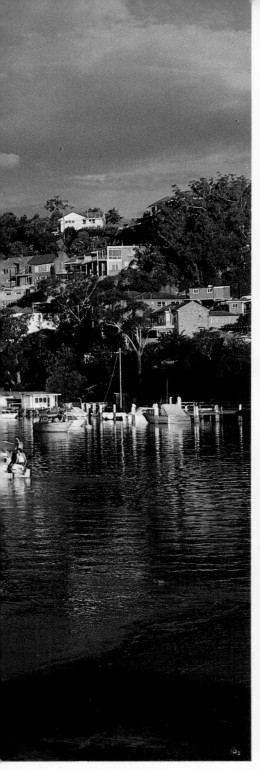

The varied scenes on these pages include Long Bay, Sydney above, its tranquility contrasting with the activity at the start of the Sydney-Hobart yacht race left.

Below is shown Spit Bridge, Sydney, and top right Rushcutters Bay.

A firework display turns the night sky over Sydney into a fairyland centre right and the scene at Pittwater, Sydney, right reveals once more the charm and serenity of this particular part of the countryside.

The magnificent aerial view overleaf shows the vast sprawl of modern Sydney.

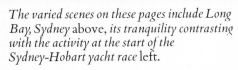

23

Sydney is extremely fortunate in having about thirty ocean beaches and a climate that makes the enjoyment of their facilities possible.

The picture top left shows one such beach, at Narabeen, and the scene centre left was taken on a beach, the name of which —Bondi —comes to mind whenever famous beaches are mentioned.

Dwarfed by the gigantic rollers that are a feature of the area, a surfer below right enjoys the unique exhilaration of this sport.

Australians are very keen on all outdoor activities and life saving and surf boat competitions are a feature of Australia's beaches every summer. Such competitions have their serious side, however, for with such ideal surfing and swimming facilities there are still accidents and highly-trained lifesavers are necessary.

The space and beauty of Whale Beach, Sydney, is exemplified by the panoramic view overleaf.

The coastline of New South Wales is one of infinite variety. The beaches, such as Bondi below, *Manley* top right *and* Coogee *below* right, *are legendary and are a great attraction for residents and visitors alike. All these beaches are cleansed each day by the pounding surf of the ocean and thus alway appear clean and fresh.*

In addition to the famous pleasure beaches, New South Wales has its share of quiet and restful coastal areas. The isolation of Seal Rocks is apparent in the picture above as is the rugged nature of the coast at Kiama top left.

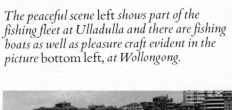

The peaceful scene left shows part of the fishing fleet at Ulladulla and there are fishing boats as well as pleasure craft evident in the picture bottom left, at Wollongong.

Australian sheep stations vary in size from about 10,000 acres to huge holdings measuring hundreds of square miles. Many of them are very isolated and even the main buildings may be several miles from main roads. Water conservation schemes and fencing form two of the main expenses on large stations; there can be hundreds of miles of fencing and, of course, without water there would be no pasture for the animals. Many of the sheep stations welcome visitors for day tours, or longer, and horse riding is a popular pastime for such visitors.

Immigrants brought their knowledge of wine growing to Australia many years ago and there are now a number of areas where grapes are cultivated for wine making, such as in the lush Hunter Valley above and bottom left.

All outdoor sports and pursuits are popular in Australia, and fishing is no exception. The rivers and lakes are plentifully stocked with fish, to the obvious delight of anglers right.

Restored or re-created settlements may be seen in many parts of Australia pictures left and below.

Thousands of locals and visitors enjoy watching horse racing such as the annual Gold Cup at Wagga Wagga in New South Wales above.

Rodeos right on the American style (complete with Australian cowboys) are big attractions in many country centres.

35

Pictured above left *is the Sydney-Newcastle Expressway and* below left *Broken Hill, called the Silver City. Its silver mines are among the world's largest.*

Lightning Ridge *above, 474 miles north west of Sydney, is the only known source in the world of the coveted black opal. Spoil from the mines creates a 'moonscape'.*

Areas of the Great Dividing Range in New South Wales are densely wooded right. *Walking tracks take over where roads end.*

Old gold diggings are shown far right *at Rocky River, near Uralla, New South Wales.*

Below is 'Booloominbah' – the University of New England's administrative buildings, at Armidale.

Parts of New South Wales are semi-arid – but when it does rain the desert blossoms overleaf.

Melbourne is the capital of Victoria, Australia's smallest mainland state. It is the country's biggest city – after Sydney – and its main financial centre; many major companies have their headquarters in the busy, tree-lined streets where modern buildings are mixed with those of the Victorian age.

Across the Yarra River from Princes Bridge is the dome of the city's main railway station above, Flinders Street, with its famous Victorian façade now dwarfed by modern commercial buildings.

The city is pictured left in the eerie half-light of dusk.

Victoria's National Gallery below houses Australia's foremost art collection.

The picture above right vividly captures the glamour of a performance of 'The Merry Widow' at the Palais Theatre.

Royal Arcade right is just one of the many Victorian shopping arcades that still survive and thrive in the modern city.

One of Australia's main ports, Melbourne is built on the flat shores of Port Phillip Bay, with garden suburbs sprawling for mile after mile. Melbournians love festivals. The Royal Show top left is primarily a display of the state's agricultural power, but there are also plenty of other attractions for the children.

At the city's annual Moomba festival left and below left there are imaginative floats and impressive parades, and at Christmas, which comes in the Australian mid-summer, Santa Claus wears a lightweight outfit but is doubtless still hot behind his traditional beard above.

Puffing Billy above right chugs through the Dandenong Ranges near Melbourne, a steam-age delight for today's youngsters.

Sovereign Hill below and below right is a re-creation of the gold mining town of Ballarat as it was in the 1850's.

Wilson's Promontory, Victoria overleaf, the southernmost part of the Australian mainland, is a National Park, where emus, kangaroos and koalas may be seen in their natural state and where there are splendid facilities for the outdoor life so beloved of Australians.

As has been shown in all manner of competitions all over the world, most kinds of sport are taken very seriously in Australia. This is, of course, partly due to the splendid climate which affords such excellent opportunities.

Horse racing is pictured top left at Flemington and left centre are shown participants in a surf boat race at Ocean Grove, Victoria.

The famous Melbourne Cricket Ground is the venue for Australian Rules Football top and cricket bottom left, while tennis is featured in the photograph above, taken at Kooyong.

On some golf courses a kangaroo might be a critical spectator, as at Anglesea golf course below.

Horse riding bottom is a popular method of relaxation on many country properties and on the coasts there are fine facilities for sailing, as right on Port Phillip Bay.

A country as vast as Australia affords a great diversity in climate. In addition to glorious, sun-drenched beaches and the blistering heat of the outback there are the extensive snowfields of the Great Dividing Range which include Mount Buller left, right and below and Falls Creek bottom left where many thousands of people take advantage of the excellent snow sports facilities.

At Mount Hotham a helicopter bottom serves as an unusual ski-lift.

The Snowy Mountains are part of the Australian Alps and are a series of steep ridges, the highest of which, at 2,230 metres, is Mount Kosciusko bottom right, an area which is highly developed for snow sports.

Mount Buller, which is also featured overleaf lies 150 miles from Melbourne and is the largest of the ski resorts in Victoria's Alps.

49

Victoria has a population of over three and a half million, but most people – more than two and a half million – live in Melbourne, the capital city. There are forecasts that the metropolitan area population will reach five to six million by the turn of the century. Further development is likely to be spurred by an abundance of energy – the state has enormous brown coal deposits, and oilfields off the eastern coast supply some 60 per cent of Australia's annual crude oil needs. Most of Victoria falls within the warm temperate belt of the southeast corner of Australia and the summers are unusually long and hot – conditions that are ideal for wine growing, as at Chateau Tahbilk, one of the cellars of which is shown *top left*.

In a creek at Buchan *left* panning for gold still continues, and *bottom left* a blacksmith still carries on his trade in the authentic pioneer settlement of Swan Hill, in the north of the state.

The scene of sheep droving *below* was taken at 'Lyndhurst', near Kilmore, and the lighthouse *above* at Port Fairy is now preserved by the National Trust. A round-up of cattle is shown *right* at 'Merrijig' property.

The great variety of countryside and the wildlife it supports, such as the Ibis' above, the prehistoric-looking 'bearded dragon' right and the galah – a type of parrot common to most parts of Australia far right – as well as such strange native Australian plants as the 'blackboy' below are well illustrated on these pages.

Looking every inch a real live 'teddy bear' the koala left is a symbol of Australia that is recognised the world over. In fact, this charming arboreal creature of eastern Australia is not a bear at all, but a marsupial of the Phalangeridae family. It reaches a height of between two to three feet and feeds, fastidiously, on eucalyptus leaves. At one time koalas were hunted and killed for their fur but they are now rigidly protected and their numbers may even be increasing.

The elegant black swan above, the emblem of Western Australia, was photographed in Melbourne's Botanic Gardens, where the picture right was also taken.

Many of Australia's native mammals are marsupials – a term meaning that the young are born at a very early stage of embryonic development and are then reared in a pouch – and another example of such an animal is the possum below.

At Healesville Sanctuary, near Melbourne, visitors talk to a cockatoo above right – which might even talk back – and make friends with a tame kangaroo bottom right.

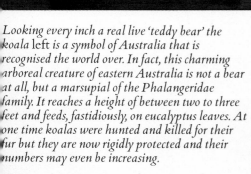

The relentless pounding of Bass Strait waves over the centuries has worn Victoria's coastline into a variety of spectacular natural arches and stacks. Many of these formations have been given names, some of which are fairly obvious, such as 'London Bridge' above, and some not so obvious, like 'The Apostles' right. Both of these examples are at Port Campbell.

Tasmania is a state apart from the rest of
Australia in more ways than one. It is an island
which has the highest rainfall, more mountains
and fewer people than any other state of the
Commonwealth. Tasmania is slightly smaller
than Ireland and has a population of 409,000
and an annual influx of some half million tourists
from the mainland and overseas.

The ruins of the early convict settlement at Port
Arthur are shown above.

Fishing boats lie in the sun-warmed waters of
Hobart's Constitution Dock above right, right
and below.

Launceston, on the northern coast, is Tasmania's
second city left and contains many imposing
churches.

MILTON HALL

60

CHESTERMAN & CO.
EDWARDS & CO.

Visitors to Tasmania may find it strange that such a beautiful island should once have been so dreaded as one of the worst prison settlements to be found anywhere. This was in the days when the island was known as Van Dieman's Land.

The west and northwest of Tasmania has rugged coastline broken by quiet bays above left. Burnie centre left is the site of a large paper industry and Coles Bay below left, which lies on the east coast, has snowy-white beaches, rocky pools and cliffs.

Hobart, the State capital, was the first city in Australia to legalise casino gambling. The tower of the Wrest Point hotel/casino complex is shown in the centre of the picture above. Hobart's Derwent estuary is spanned by the Tasman Bridge below, and the sprawl of the city along the shores of the estuary is shown right, from Mount Wellington.

Queensland is the Australia of the imagination —
vast, open spaces with huge cattle and sheep runs,
bananas and oranges in back gardens, houses on
stilts, seemingly endless tropical beaches and sun-
tanned people with a relaxed life-style.

Brisbane right is a rambling, evergreen city built
on the banks of the Brisbane River about twenty-
five miles from the sea. It lies only a few degrees
south of the Tropic of Capricorn and it is a city of
fine buildings and colourful parks and gardens.

Brisbane's Storey Bridge is transformed by the
sunset above into a delicate filigree of steel.

In contrast to the modern, high rise and floodlit
buildings left is Brisbane Town Hall below.

The sprawling metropolis of Brisbane is pictured
overleaf.

With its mile after mile of perfect beaches, including ocean surf beaches for thrills and spills in surf boats and on surf boards, Queensland is rightly known as the 'sunshine state'.

Although the sea offers a tremendous variety of enjoyment and excitement it can also be dangerous and all main beaches are patrolled by lifesavers whose clubs hold annual beach carnivals and competitions. One such event takes place at Burleigh Heads below right.

Surfers Paradise overleaf and on pages 72 and 73 is the principal centre of a twenty mile chain of beaches and surfing resorts south of Brisbane.

73

There is much to see and do along Queensland's Gold Coast. Trained dolphins go through their elaborate routines and there are performances by highly skilled water skiers at Sea World *left* and there are always beaches where not another person may be in sight. Some idea of the size of Australia may be gathered from the fact that this one state – Queensland – is as large as the whole of France, West Germany, Belgium, Holland, Switzerland, Denmark, Italy and Spain put together.

An endearing colony of koalas is pictured overleaf at Lone Pine Sanctuary near Brisbane.

Koalas are a delight for the children, who invariably love having their pictures taken with the 'teddy bears'. Being nocturnal creatures they are particularly sleepy and cuddly during the day and at places such as the Lone Pine Sanctuary they are quite used to people.

Thousands of lorikeets and parakeets are a great attraction at the Currumbin Bird Sanctuary on the Gold Coast.

Trail riding is a popular part of a visit to most parts of Australia overleaf.

79

Cairns and islands off the northern Queensland coast provide bases for big game fishing. Of 48 salt water game species listed by the International Game Fishing Association, 26 are found in Australian waters. Cairns Game Fishing Club below and right is a mecca for big game fishermen from all over the world.

Islands of the Great Barrier Reef were first charted by Britain's Captain James Cook, who named many of them. Overleaf is pictured the famous Whitsunday Passage.

The Great Barrier Reef of Australia is considered to be one of nature's masterpieces. It runs parallel to the coast along the northeastern shore of Queensland and it is a marine enthusiast's paradise. It provides a unique opportunity for underwater study, being inhabited by thousands of different species of sea creatures. Some of the islands of the Great Barrier Reef are pictured on these pages. Horse riding on Dunk Island is shown left, Michaelmas Cay above and Heron Island right and below.

Pictured on these pages is Heron Island above and the mysterious beauty of the underwater world of the Great Barrier Reef.

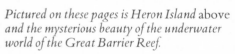

In Queensland's immense 'Outback', beef, lamb and wool are big industries. Nearly all of Australia's sugar, pineapple and peanuts and nearly half its tobacco is produced in this area. There are miles of orange groves and banana plantations, all producing considerable revenues.

Queensland's immense diversity is well illustrated by the pictures on these pages which range from cattle droving top left, to a dusty race meeting on the dry plains centre left and an outback rodeo bottom left.

On a riverside above grows a flowering 'bottle brush' tree while the harvest is gathered on a tobacco plantation below.

The fantastic formation of a fig tree is shown right, deep in the heart of a tropical rain forest.

Eucla is near the border of Western and South Australia, on the Eyre Highway which links Perth with eastern cities. The ruins of an old telegraph station overleaf stand starkly against the glorious sunset. To the south of Eucla is the Great Australian Bight; to the north lies the vast emptiness of the Nullarbor – meaning 'no trees' – Plain and the Great Victorian Desert.

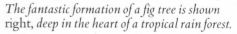

Australia is known all over the world for the extent and variety of its wildlife. Above is the rare, migratory Cape Barren Goose and top left, in detailed close-up, the tawny frogmouth, a well-named nocturnal creature. The tiger snake left centre is variable in colour and pattern but, whatever its markings, its venom remains deadly. The flightless bird below left is the emu and next to it, bottom is the laughing kookaburra. The little creature pictured below is the wombat and right are two animals found, in their wild state, only in Australia: the kangaroo below right and the almost unbelievable Platypus, or duckbill, right.

Pelicans and black swans contentedly share an outback lagoon overleaf.

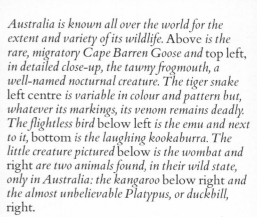

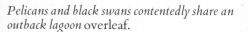

Adelaide below and left *is big enough to be a city but small enough to escape the problems of a large metropolis. It is a city of wide streets, many parks and a large number of fine churches. There is a handy golf course* above *near the centre of the city, allowing lunchtime practice sessions.*

The Kangaroos right *were photographed in Cleland Conservation Park, in the Mount Lofty Ranges, about twenty minutes' drive from Adelaide.*

South Australia is the driest of all the Australian states. To the north, bordering on Central Australia, are great areas of sand dune and desert overleaf.

Adelaide contains many fine restaurants and it may be that the abundant local wine was partly responsible for their development for, only about an hour's drive from Adelaide lies the beginning of the Barossa Valley, Australia's greatest wine producing area, responsible for the production of some 70 per cent of Australia's fine table wines for both home consumption and export. Adelaide and South Australia are famous for two festivals – the Adelaide Arts Festival which takes place in even years and the Barossa Valley Vintage Wine Festival above left, at which a huge maypole is erected, held during odd years. The Barossa Valley was settled in 1839 by refugees from Germany, who brought with them both their wine-making skills and their customs.

At Mount Gambier, on the borders of South Australia and Victoria, lies the remarkable Blue Lake top right, in the crater of an extinct volcano.

The fantastic geological formations below right are in the northern Flinders Ranges.

Much of the interior of Australia contains primitive landscapes, made more apparent by their remoteness and the fact that they have been virtually untouched by civilisation. With almost no buildings to be seen it is not difficult to imagine this land almost unchanged since the dawn of history.

Katherine Gorge left *is a spectacular feature of the Northern Territory about 220 miles south of Darwin, and* Ormiston Gorge *above lies 80 miles west of Alice Springs in Central Australia.*

In Standley Chasm *below, the 200 feet high cliffs are only a mere twelve feet apart in places and the cliff faces glow bright red in the midday sun.*

Ayers Rock right and overleaf *is a giant monolith 210 miles southwest of Alice Springs. A place of Aboriginal mystery and legend, Ayers Rock is the tip of a mountain, fallen on its side. Visitors can stay overnight at nearby lodges in order to see the dramatic colour changes that take place at sunset and dawn.*

Darwin above has been completely rebuilt since it was devastated by a cyclone on Christmas Eve, 1974.

Australia's largest bird, the emu, is pictured left.

Outback tracks below in the Northern Territory.

A typical outback Northern Territory homestead, complete with its own landing strip is shown right.

Ross River, an outback resort overleaf, was once part of a 'station' which bred horses for the British Army in India.

Alice Springs above is almost in the geographical centre of Australia and sporting events such as rodeos below and the Camel Cup above right are popular in the area.

Kings Canyon top left is about 140 miles west of Alice Springs and the wierd domes of Mount Olga centre left are close to Ayers Rock.

Pitchi-Richi Bird Sanctuary, on the outskirts of Alice Springs, contains a collection of Aboriginal sculptures by Victorian artist William Ricketts bottom left.

A river with no water – bottom – is the dried-up bed of the Todd River, which flows but infrequently.

The sparse vegetation and loneliness of the Australian Outback is shown below right and overleaf: Macdonnell Ranges are among the oldest mountains on earth.

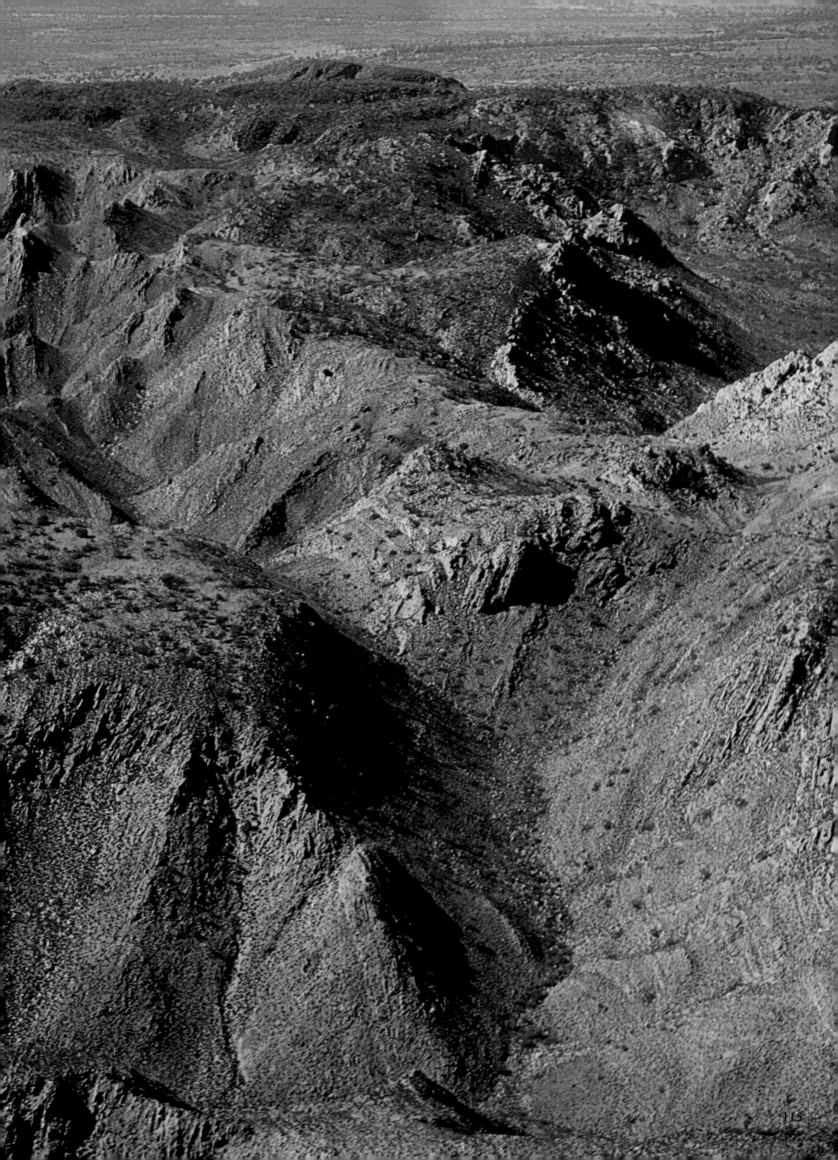

An Aboriginal camp is pictured above in the Alice Springs area, and a banana plantation below on Elcho Island off the northern tip of the Northern Territory.

Australia's Aboriginals are first class horsemen right.

Camels left were first imported into Australia by early explorers and settlers. Many of their descendants still roam wild.

117

Groote Eylandt *left was named by a Dutch explorer who discovered the Northern Territory coast in 1623. The Aboriginal women shown here are collecting shellfish.*

Aboriginals in Arnhem Land above and below *live in their tribal state, hunting fish with spears, collecting eggs and preparing and roasting wallabies or small kangaroos* bottom right. *An Aboriginal cowboy is shown* centre right, *and* top right *a rarely-photographed Aboriginal ceremony.*

The immensity of the Outback, its mystery and Aboriginal legend, are typified by this shot of the Olgas overleaf, *near Ayers Rock in Central Australia.*

119

Western Australia is the country's biggest state, occupying about a million square miles, or a third of the Continent, and it has just over a million inhabitants. Perth, the State capital, has been described as one of the most isolated major cities on earth and it rejoices in the claim of being Australia's sunniest city. The city is featured centre left *across the Swan River. The building* above left *is Winthrop Hall, Perth University* and above *is the entrance to London Court, an* arcade in the heart of the city. The Round House bottom left *is the oldest building in Western* Australia.

The boab below — *or, more correctly, the baobab* tree — found in Western Australia, is often called a 'bottle tree' because of its distinctive shape. There are spectacular limestone caves at Augusta, 186 miles from Perth. This one top right *is called the* 'jewel cave'. Lake Argyle bottom right, *on the* Ord River is part of a multi-million dollar irrigation project.

The wierd shapes overleaf *are variously called* 'the Pinnacles', 'the Sculptures' or even 'the Tombstones'. They consist of hardened deposits of lime and silica.

Western Australia is also known as the 'State of Excitement' and it contains a great and varied wealth of scenery. The state is also incredibly rich in mineral deposits, including enough iron ore to feed the blast furnaces of the world for generations. This iron ore is so plentiful that pieces of rock picked up from the ground can be welded together. There are big nickel mines and what has been guardedly described as a 'significant' uranium find. There are billions of cubic metres of gas reserves off the north west coast and several alumina projects. It is said that Western Australia could well become Australia's first nuclear state. Mining operations are so big, and the amount of money involved is so huge, that the state's primary productions, including wool, meat, dairy products and other items tend to get overlooked.

Pearling luggers top centre and right *operate from Broome, to the north of Western Australia.*

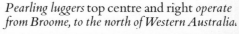

One of Western Australia's most popular surfing beaches is Scarborough Beach top, far left, near Perth.

The strange formation far left centre on Lake Argyle is known as Elephant Rock.

Mount Meharry far left bottom is situated in the iron-rich Hammersley Ranges above, which contain the world's largest known deposits of iron ore.

Pictured below left is Dales Gorge, also in the Hammersley Range.

The abandoned mine workings below are at Leonora, northeast of Perth.

First published in Great Britain 1979 by Colour Library International Ltd.
© Illustrations: Colour Library International Ltd, 163 East 64th St., New York, N.Y. 10021
Colour separations by Fercrom, Barcelona, Spain.
Display and text filmsetting by Focus Photoset, London, England.
Printed and bound by Rieusset, Barcelona, Spain.
All rights reserved.
ISBN 0-8317-0591-4 Library of Congress Catalogue Card No. 79-2147
Published in the United States of America by Mayflower Books, Inc., New York City
Published in Canada by Wm. Collins and Sons, Toronto